Drawing Is Fun!

DRAWING
SEA CREATURES

Gareth Stevens
Publishing

Please visit our website, www.garethstevens.com. For a free color catalog of all our high-quality books, call toll free 1-800-542-2595 or fax 1-877-542-2596.

Library of Congress Cataloging-in-Publication Data

Clunes, Rebecca.
Drawing sea creatures / Rebecca Clunes.
    p. cm. — (Drawing is fun)
Includes index.
ISBN 978-1-4339-5948-6 (pbk.)
ISBN 978-1-4339-5949-3 (6-pack)
ISBN 978-1-4339-5946-2 (library binding)
1. Marine animals in art—Juvenile literature. 2. Drawing—Technique—Juvenile literature. I. Title.
NC781.C58 2011
743.6—dc22

                            2010052707

First Edition

Published in 2012 by
Gareth Stevens Publishing
111 East 14th Street, Suite 349
New York, NY 10003

Copyright © 2012 Arcturus Publishing

Cartoon illustrations: Dynamo Limited
Text: Rebecca Clunes and Dynamo Limited
Editors: Anna Brett, Kate Overy, and Joe Harris
Design: Tokiko Morishima
Cover design: Tokiko Morishima

Picture credits: All images supplied by Shutterstock, except page 18 (iStockphoto); and page 22 (Amos Nachoum/CORBIS).

Printed in China

CPSIA compliance information: Batch # AS11GS: For further information contact Gareth Stevens, New York, New York at 1-800-542-2595.

SL001843US

Contents

Clown Fish

This clown fish lives in warm seas.

He is brightly colored, with orange and white stripes.

He is about three inches (8 cm) long.

He has a special slime on his body. The slime keeps him from getting stung by sea anemones.

FUN FACTS ● FUN FACTS ● FUN FACTS ● FUN FACTS ● FUN FACTS

Clown fish look after their eggs until the babies hatch out.

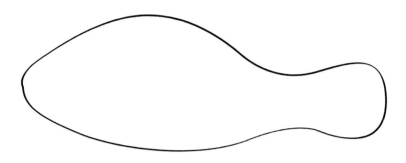

1. Begin with this fishy body shape.

2. Add the fins and an eye.

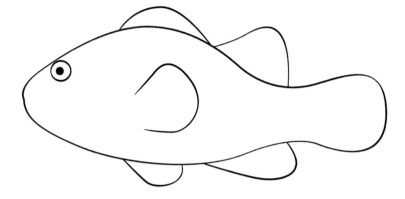

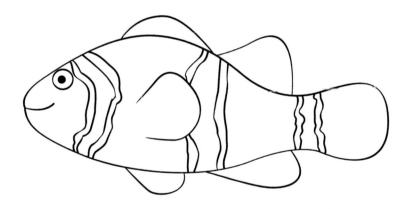

3. Draw some wavy lines for the stripes.

4. Draw some extra, thinner lines on the fins. Then color your fish in.

Turtle

This turtle breathes air but she spends most of her life in the water.

She has a hard shell on her back.

She swims with her four flippers.

Some turtles eat crabs, jellyfish, and snails. Others just eat seaweed.

FUN FACTS ● FUN FACTS ● FUN FACTS ● FUN FACTS ● FUN FACTS

Turtles lay their eggs on sandy beaches and then swim away. The baby turtles find their own way to the sea.

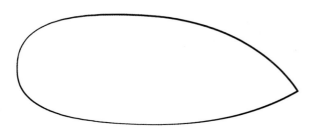

1. Start with this oval shape.

2. Divide it in half to make the shell, then add the head.

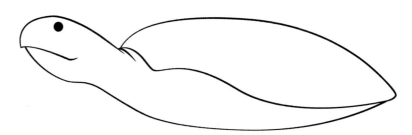

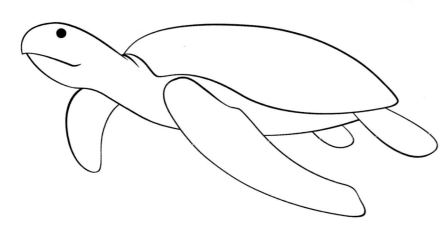

3. Add flippers to the front and back of the body.

4. Add some spots to her skin, then color her in.

Killer whale

This killer whale has a black body with white patches.

He has a fin on his back.

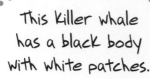

He has sharp teeth. He eats fish, birds, and sea lions.

His tail moves up and down when he swims.

FUN FACTS ● FUN FACTS ● FUN FACTS ● FUN FACTS ● FUN FACTS

Killer whales live with their families. There are about 20 killer whales in each group.

1. This long shape makes up most of the body.

2. Draw in the tail and fin.

3. The front fins finish off the main shape.

4. Draw the white patches in carefully, then color the rest of the body black.

Seahorse

This seahorse is a type of fish.

She swims by moving the fin on her back.

She sucks up her food with her mouth.

She has a tail she can curl around plants.

FUN FACTS ● FUN FACTS ● FUN FACTS ● FUN FACTS ● FUN FACTS

The mother seahorse gives her eggs to the father seahorse. He looks after the eggs until the babies hatch.

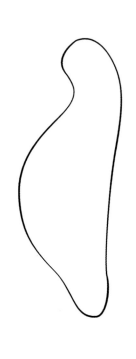

1. This curved shape makes up the body.

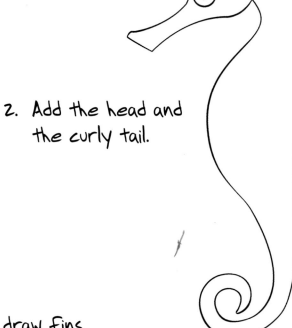

2. Add the head and the curly tail.

3. Next, draw fins on the head and the back.

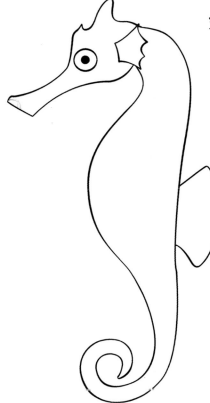

4. Don't forget the spiky mane down the seahorse's neck.

Walrus

This walrus is very fat. This keeps him warm in the cold sea.

He has long tusks.

His back flippers are strong to push him through the water. He steers with his front flippers.

He is big, about 14 feet (4.3 meters) long.

FUN FACTS ● FUN FACTS ● FUN FACTS ● FUN FACTS ● FUN FACTS

Walruses are good swimmers. They dive down to the ocean floor and eat the small animals they find there.

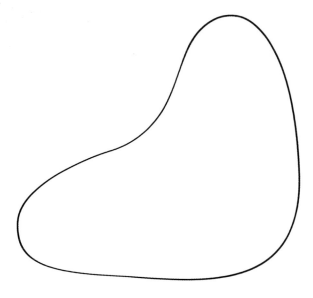

1. Draw a large blob for the body.

2. Add a round, smiling face.

3. Draw long tusks, then begin his flippers.

4. Finish off the flippers, then color your walrus.

Jellyfish

This jellyfish has a soft, wobbly body.

The top of the jellyfish is called the bell.

The jellyfish does not have eyes, ears, or a brain.

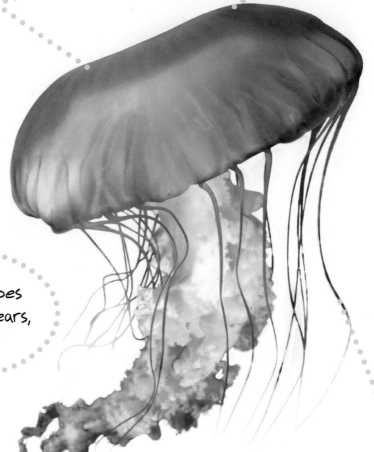

The tentacles look like hair—but they can sting!

FUN FACTS ● FUN FACTS ● FUN FACTS ● FUN FACTS ● FUN FACTS

Some jellyfish can sting even after they have died.

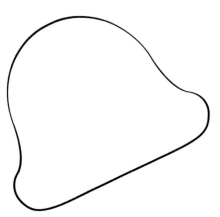

1. A basic bell shape begins the body.

2. Draw some curves along the bottom.

3. Add lots of wavy tentacles for catching prey.

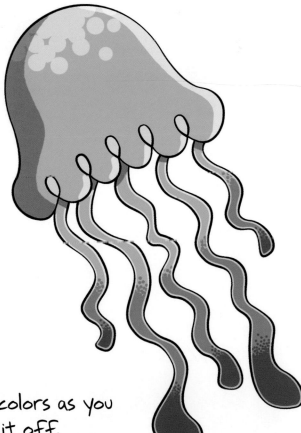

4. Use as many colors as you like to finish it off.

Sea otter

This sea otter has brown fur.

Her thick fur keeps her warm in the water.

She closes her ears and nose under the water.

She eats animals with hard shells. She puts the shell on her tummy, then bangs it with a rock until it opens.

FUN FACTS ● FUN FACTS ● FUN FACTS ● FUN FACTS ● FUN FACTS

Before they sleep, sea otters wrap seaweed around their tummies. This keeps them from floating away.

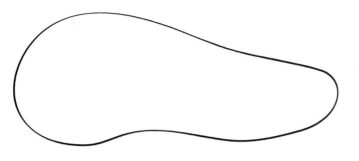

1. A squashed blob is the starting point for the otter's body.

2. Add the head, the tail, and a small dot for the eye.

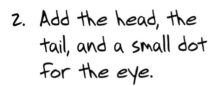

3. Next add two legs.

4. Give her two more legs, small ears, a nose, and some whiskers.

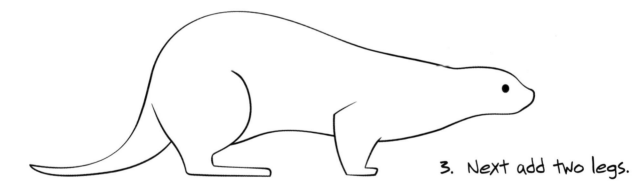

Sailfish

This sailfish can swim at up to 70 miles (113 km) an hour.

The shape of his body means he can slip through the water very quickly.

He eats fish and squid.

Sailfish live in warm seas all over the world.

FUN FACTS ● FUN FACTS ● FUN FACTS ● FUN FACTS ● FUN FACTS

Female sailfish lay millions of eggs, but many animals eat them. Only a few will grow into adult sailfish.

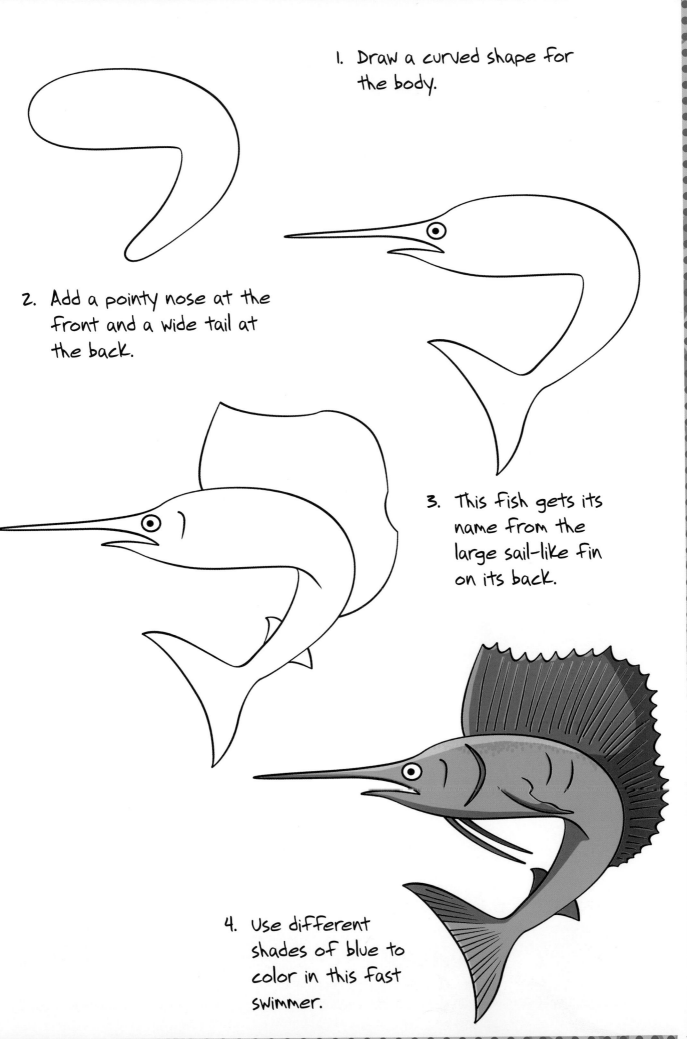

1. Draw a curved shape for the body.

2. Add a pointy nose at the front and a wide tail at the back.

3. This fish gets its name from the large sail-like fin on its back.

4. Use different shades of blue to color in this fast swimmer.

Lobster

This lobster has a strong shell.

She has eight legs for walking.

She catches crabs, worms, and snails with her claws.

She uses her antennae to search for food and look out for danger.

FUN FACTS ● FUN FACTS ● FUN FACTS ● FUN FACTS ● FUN FACTS

Lobsters live a long time. Some lobsters can live to be 100 years old.

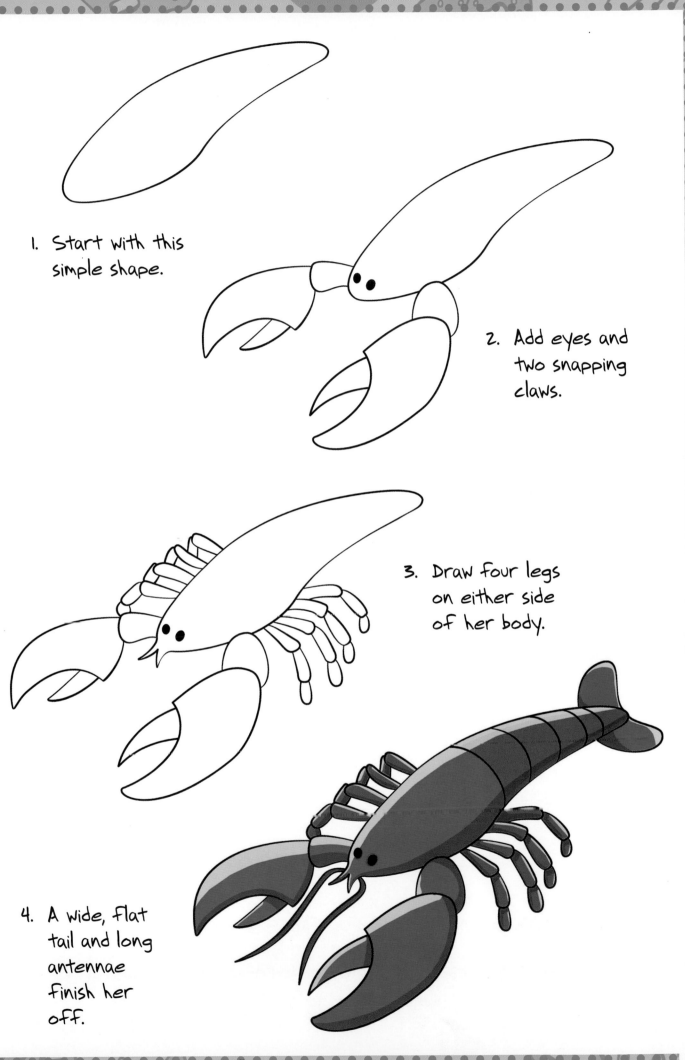

1. Start with this simple shape.

2. Add eyes and two snapping claws.

3. Draw four legs on either side of her body.

4. A wide, flat tail and long antennae finish her off.

Hammerhead shark

This hammerhead shark has an eye on either side of his "hammer."

He sometimes swims in a group with other hammerheads.

He eats fish, small sharks, and stingrays.

He is 20 feet (6 meters) long.

FUN FACTS ● FUN FACTS ● FUN FACTS ● FUN FACTS ● FUN FACTS

Why do these sharks have weird-shaped heads? The hammer helps them to see in all directions.

1. Draw a simple curved shape for the body.

2. Add a tail and a hammer-shaped head.

3. Wide, flat fins make him look more like a shark.

4. Color him in dark blue or gray.

23

Octopus

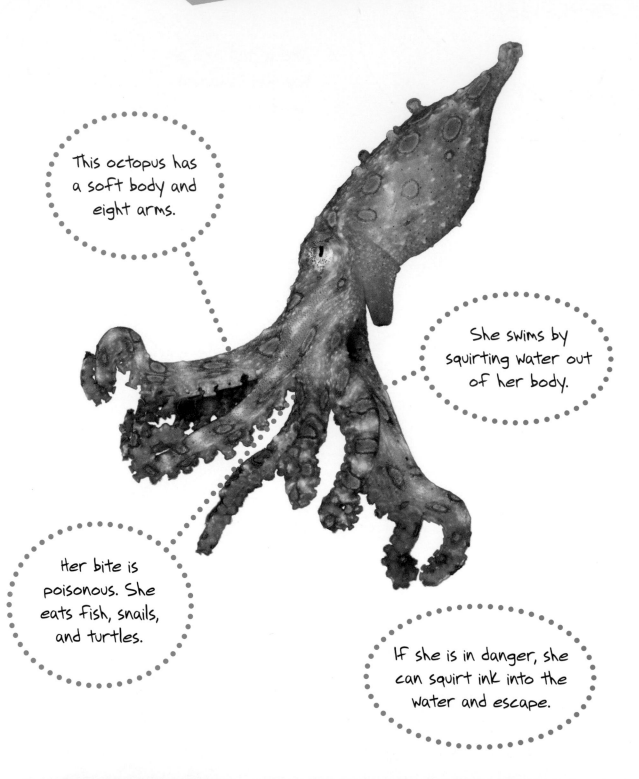

This octopus has a soft body and eight arms.

She swims by squirting water out of her body.

Her bite is poisonous. She eats fish, snails, and turtles.

If she is in danger, she can squirt ink into the water and escape.

FUN FACTS ● FUN FACTS ● FUN FACTS ● FUN FACTS ● FUN FACTS

The blue-ringed octopus lives in Australia. Its bite can kill a person in just a few minutes.

1. This shape gives you the body and two arms.

2. Add two eyes and more arms.

3. Draw still more arms—you need eight in total.

4. Add suckers on the arms. Then color her in any way you want.

Sea lion

She eats fish, crabs, and lobsters.

This sea lion is a type of seal.

She turns her back flippers forward on the land. This helps her to walk.

She can move quickly on land—and even faster in the water.

FUN FACTS ● FUN FACTS ● FUN FACTS ● FUN FACTS ● FUN FACTS

Young sea lions are called pups. They stay with their mother for at least a year.

1. This squashed egg shape makes the body.

2. Give her a head and a tail.

3. Draw the front and back flippers.

4. Add the whiskers and then color her brown or gray.

Stingray

This stingray has a large, flat body.

He swims by flapping his sides. It looks a bit like a bird flying.

His eyes are on top of his head but his mouth and nose are underneath.

He has a poisonous spine on his tail.

FUN FACTS ● FUN FACTS ● FUN FACTS ● FUN FACTS ● FUN FACTS

Stingrays live at the bottom of the sea. They hide on the sea floor if they are in danger.

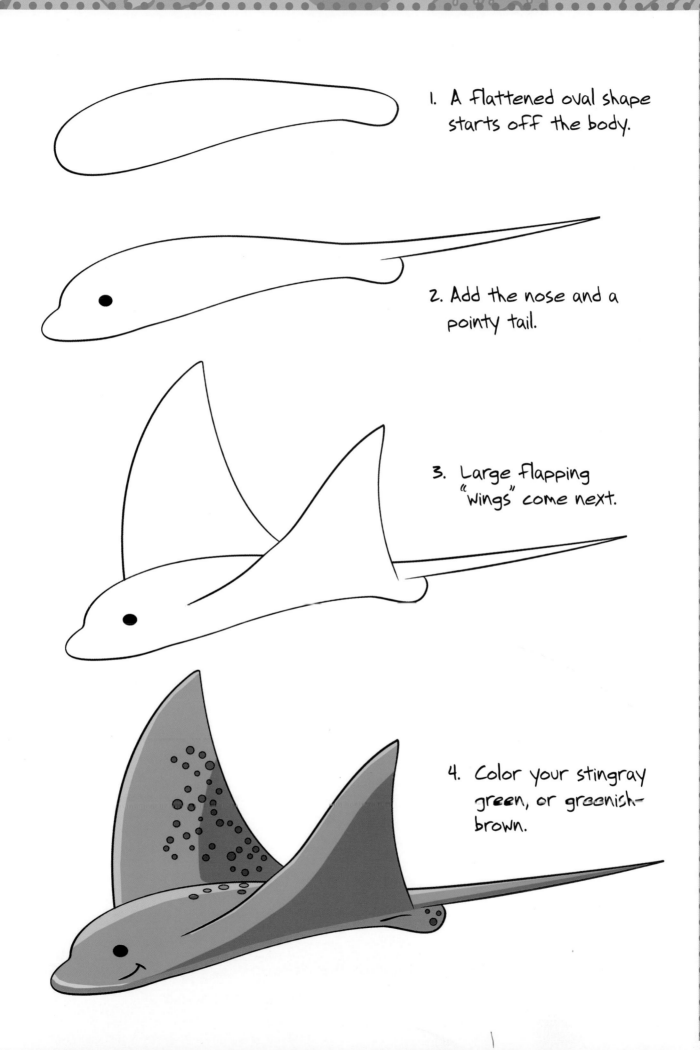

1. A flattened oval shape starts off the body.

2. Add the nose and a pointy tail.

3. Large flapping "wings" come next.

4. Color your stingray green, or greenish-brown.

Crab

This crab has eight legs and two claws.

She has a hard shell.

If she loses a leg, she can grow it back.

She walks sideways.

FUN FACTS ● FUN FACTS ● FUN FACTS ● FUN FACTS ● FUN FACTS

The smallest crab is only the size of a pea. The largest crab is 12 feet (3.7 meters) wide.

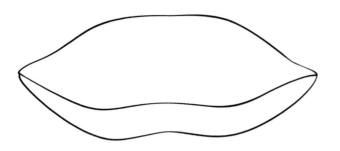

1. Draw a shape that looks like a pair of lips.

2. Add some eyes and two big snapping claws.

3. Draw four back legs. You can't see all of the crab's legs in this picture.

4. Use orange and brown to finish off your picture.

Glossary

antennae the feelers on top of an animal's head used for smelling and touching

fin a thin, flat part of an animal's body, used for pushing it through the water or for steering

flipper a wide, flat part of an animal, used to help it swim

poisonous contains a liquid that kills or injures an animal

sea anemone an animal that sticks to a rock and looks like a flower. It eats fish and has stinging tentacles.

shell a hard covering for an animal's body that protects it

slime a thick, slippery liquid

spine a thin, pointy spike sticking out from an animal's body

squirt to shoot out a stream of water

suckers round pads that can stick to things

tentacles long, bendable legs, such as the legs of an octopus

tusks the long, pointy teeth that stick out from an animal's mouth

Further Reading

Brecke, Nicole, and Patricia M. Stockland. *Sea Creatures You Can Draw*. Millbrook Press, 2010.

Levin, Freddie. *1-2-3 Draw Ocean Life*. Peel, 2005.

Soloff-Levy, Barbara. *How to Draw Aquarium Animals*. Dover Publications, 2003.

Index